MODERN SPIRITUALITY

The Power of Balanced Living

Holistic Lifestyle
High-Tech Meditation

Master Charles Cannon

with Will Wilkinson

Also by, about or based on the work of Master Charles Cannon:

The Bliss of Freedom
A Contemporary Mystic's Enlightening Journey

The Meditation Toolbox

The Modern Mystic
Quotations

Forgiving the Unforgivable
The Power of Holistic Living

ISBN Number   978-1-884068-73-7

Printed and published by Synchronicity Foundation
P.O. Box 694
Nellysford, VA 22958 USA
434.361.2323   800.962.2033
www.synchronicity.org

Printed in Canada

This book is dedicated to

balance and wholeness…

the fulfillment of being human.

Table of Contents

Preface

Fulfillment is what we all want. It takes different shapes for each of us, but in one way or another fulfillment means that our experience of life becomes consistently enjoyable. It seems to take many years of frustrating effort for most people to finally admit that this doesn't come from the outside. Likewise, searching within - while ignoring the practicalities of life - proves dangerously impractical.

Balance is the key. The great wisdom traditions, surviving from ancient times and cultures, all present similar, timeless principles to support achieving a consistently balanced life experience, and meditation is universally recommended to deepen one's connection with the source of life, classically referred to as God. In fact, countless studies have indicated that meditation remains the most effective transformative practice to support personal evolution and fulfillment. Meditation disciplines the unruly mind, while a range of other disciplines and practices are taught to transform one's external experience from stressful chaos into dependable order.

Traditionally, the serious seeker was required to abandon family, friends, and almost every aspect of a "normal" lifestyle. The deepest levels of fulfillment could only be attained through personal contact with an acknowledged master and within the confines of structured, monastic communities which existed separate and distinct from society. This way of life only appealed to those few who were willing, able and prepared to endure its rigors.

Today, increasing numbers of people have become frustrated with their lives and are actively seeking the fulfillment that has eluded them. But a housewife with three children cannot drop everything to join an ashram. The business owner with scores of employees and a looming merger can't suddenly move to India. Students struggling with antiquated curriculums can't exchange their textbooks for ancient Vedic scriptures.

Happiness may be hunted in on-line social networks that turn out to offer mostly superficial, anonymous communication, or vicariously through celebrity excesses, or by praying to win the lottery or American Idol, even though the odds for success are about the same as being struck by lightning twice.

How then can modern "seekers" - who would probably never refer to themselves that way but *would* readily admit that their lives aren't working any more - come to experience fulfillment, right in the middle of this increasingly complex and fragmented world?

While advances in technology have created both incredible lifestyle benefits and a stressful environment, they have also given rise to a remarkable alternative to traditional models for exploring fulfillment. It is now possible to produce an enlightening environment without renouncing society or having direct, personal contact with an acknowledged master. A well-proven audio technology can be used to balance the two brain hemispheres during meditation and to harmonize electronic pollution in the home or office environment. Coupled with principles and practices that support the individual to develop a holistic lifestyle, and benefiting from a master's mentorship via print, audio, video and on-line, the modern seeker finally has the tools he or she needs to experience fulfillment.

This slim book introduces The Synchronicity Experience of

Modern Spirituality, pioneered by Master Charles Cannon who established Synchronicity Foundation for Modern Spirituality in 1983. Based in Virginia, Master Charles and the Foundation have been conducting research for the past twenty-eight years, developing and testing techniques for expanding and integrating what is essential for true fulfillment: "holistic awareness." The Synchronicity Experience has succeeded in helping thousands of individuals for nearly three decades to transform their lives for one simple reason: it works. It is precise and efficient, taking far less time and effort than classical systems of meditation and holistic lifestyle teachings. Accelerated changes in personal awareness have been validated by measuring brain-wave patterns. Regular participants in The Synchronicity Experience develop four times faster than others. To give readers their own direct experience, a High-Tech Meditation CD is included with this book.

As you read the following pages, you will begin exploring a comprehensive system that addresses every aspect of human experience. It is designed for the challenging times in which we live and acknowledges both the ancient, traditional models and contemporary needs. For increasing numbers of individuals, this is an experience whose time has come.

This book brings an important and timely message to our world. It is a guide to truthful experience for humanity from an authentic spiritual master. The author, Master Charles Cannon, has updated time-honored truths from the great wisdom traditions of our history into modern, contemporary language that is immediately understandable and applicable to these challenging times. Woven into the text are practical tools for actualizing these truths for yourself. You will discover a meditation technology designed specifically for this high-tech world, plus a detailed array of practices to develop a lifestyle of consistent fulfillment.

COMMENTS FROM SYNCHRONICITY ASSOCIATES

As someone who introduces this work to many and as a long-time teacher of Synchronicity students, I am delighted to have this simple reference for all who would ask the questions, "Who am I and what is life all about?" If you have ever asked these questions, this book can guide you to the answers that already live within yourself.

- Dr. Phil Duncan, Virginia

Someone once said, 'The truth is as close as the nose on your face!' My eighty-year-old life has been one constant quest for that truth. In my early years I searched outside myself. I was attracted to the Christian way and believed that through following Jesus Christ, who claimed to be ' The way, the truth and the life' that I could find what I was looking for in him, so I became an ordained priest. But I quickly found this to be far too conceptual. I needed something practical, something experiential. So, I sought the truth in my relationships. Although they were profound - at least some of them - they too seemed limited and, ultimately, unsatisfying. Next, I tried meditation but, with no one to guide me, that quickly proved unsatisfactory as well.

Eventually I was introduced to the Synchronicity High-Tech

Meditation program. Actually, I read an earlier edition of this very book that you are beginning to read now, and so I began the discipline of meditating with soundtracks and stereo headphones. I also came under the tutelage of Master Charles, whom I have found to be an authentic master of meditation. He has mentored me for the past twenty years. My quest for truth is by no means complete; that will continue to the end of my days. But my experience now is that the truth is as close as the headphones on my ears! I am content.

- Jeremy Shaw, New Zealand

I was a regular meditator for years before I contacted the Synchronicity Foundation and I'd already felt my inner fog clearing. High-Tech Meditation really accelerated that, like super-powered windshield wipers cleaning my lens of perception, on all levels.

It's all about balance. To me, balance means feeling "together", healthy, integrated, living with an inner state of calm and strength, a peace that never goes away, no matter what happens. It's like having a core that is immovable.

After the 2008 Mumbai terrorist attack, which took the lives of my husband and daughter, Master Charles and I co-founded One Life Alliance, to honor the sacredness of life and to help people learn how to live with balance and wholeness. When we honor the sacredness of life in ourselves and in each other, we make a truthful contribution to our world. I'm happy to validate this book and wish you well with your holistic explorations.

- Kia Scherr, Virginia

❧

Introduction

Thank you for choosing this book and CD. Feel free to read or listen in any order at any time, so that you can experientially understand what is offered, rather than settling for mere intellectual stimulation. You'll be able to recognize when you are actually experiencing what is presented here because you will feel it... an increase of joyfulness and an expansion of your awareness. Anticipate that this will happen; it's the intended design of these materials.

The enclosed CD is a sample of our High-Tech Meditation program, explained in a later chapter. I certainly recommend that anyone genuinely interested in a fulfilling life learn meditation, not just as an isolated practice once or twice a week, but to grow into a daily way of living. That may seem impractical, given the frantic nature of the 21st Century, but the need has never been greater – to learn how to live in balance.

Balance develops in consciousness as we become aware of and able to witness ourselves occupying a "position" between the two polarities of this dualistic world. We know many manifestations of these opposites: light and dark, stillness and action, happy and sad, etc. Living in balance is initially about consciously choosing when to return to the center from either side, while judging or worshipping neither. Any person who undertakes this experiment can discover a new kind of sustained fulfillment arising over time, just from the balancing itself, rather than from adrenaline-fed excess in the extremes.

There is a rhythm to this and we quickly discover that life is actually a "play of consciousness." It's all happening "in here." "Out there" is a reflection, uniquely and faithfully replicating the condition of our personal inner state. This explains why judgment is so detrimental and guidance is so essential. Habits of judgment and behavior, based on years of unconscious ignorance of this inner/outer, cause/effect relationship, are never given up overnight, especially surrounded as we all are by the illusion that disconnection between inner and outer is normal!

Meditating itself is not enough. In fact, it has become much more difficult to meditate in this modern era. Technology has blessed us in obvious ways but ambient electronic pollution interferes with brain function. Ironically, we've used technology to solve this problem. The enclosed High-Tech Meditation sampler welcomes you to your first-hand experience of the difference. Long-time meditators often express amazement when they first put on their headphones and close their eyes. It's simply easier to quiet your thoughts with scientifically formulated sonic entrainment. Modulating brain-wave frequencies assist the high-tech meditator to reach deeper states of equilibrium relatively quickly.

High-Tech Meditation is the centerpiece of what we call the Holistic Lifestyle, presented in two following chapters: theory and applications. You will learn how to increase and refine the quality of your personal power, how to turn the Five Principles of Holistic Living and the Five Truths of the Holistic Model into a consistently "enlightening" experience (having given up the concept of final "enlightenment"). The liberating truth is that all of us will be learning and evolving forever.

2

I invite you to begin this journey with a simple self-diagnostic. In this moment, observe the quality of your experience. What's going on as you read? None of us were taught how to tune in this way but it's easy. Just notice what's going on. Are you distracted, anxious, hopeful, curious…? Are you wanting anything -- for instance -- understanding? Are you hoping that you will do it right, worried that you might not? What would it feel like to just let all that go? Take a breath in… now let it out… and release whatever is getting in the way of simply enjoying these moments of reading. Pause for another moment, right after this word…………….

Now, reading once again, reflect on how it felt to interrupt your reading routine this way. Just observe, knowing that you are not reaching for some kind of right answer. This is just a no-rules contemplation moment that gives you a snapshot of your inner state.

This is also one simple balancing technique for finding the peaceful core which Kia spoke about in the Preface. It's here inside you, waiting like a favorite easy chair that invites you to sink deep and relax. Actually, coming to know the answers to your most important questions is not difficult when you allow new experience to grow your understanding like this. Thank you for choosing fulfillment, from the inside out. You **Can** get there from here.

Master Charles Cannon
Synchronicity Foundation
September 1, 2011

❧

Part One

Creating a Fulfilling Life

Part One
Creating a Fulfilling Life

How is it that some people are better able to create a fulfilling life than others? While there are many factors involved, one that you can do something about is the amount and quality of palatable, personal power you have at your disposal. This is not a strategy that most people consider, but the theory that we all create our own reality becomes a realistic strategy when we have the necessary power to create that reality.

It is unfortunate that many self-help books neglect to honestly inform readers that this is what is required, rather than simply reading books and attending seminars until they "get it." In ancient times, students would undertake many years of training before they achieved mastery. And they always worked with self-realized masters.

Here in the West we are in a hurry. The television remote control has become a symbol of our short attention spans and desire for instant gratification. We just click, which is something we can easily do for ourselves! And we like to be independent; in fact, many of us have authority phobia, because our leaders have let us down so often. When it comes to learning about life and creating a better one, those who put themselves forward as experts are often good communicators and promoters but don't necessarily always walk their talk (as is sadly revealed when scandals arise). We certainly have marvelous examples of those who do -- modern day heroines like Mother Teresa.

Increasing Your Personal Power

If you have ever consulted the troubleshooting guide in an electronics manual, you have probably encountered this advice: "Make sure the unit is plugged in." Actually, that's good advice for us too! What is the source of your power and are you really connected to it? This is the power that keeps your heart beating and your cells regenerating. Certainly, it is not your conscious mind that does that.

Regardless of whether you believe in God or not, there is a source of power that is sustaining your life experience. In this book, I am less interested in describing what this source is than in assisting you towards an increased conscious experience of it. I can tell you from years of experience - my own, that of my teachers, and that of my associates and students - that the essential nature of this source is bliss. When you are fully connected to this source so that it is flowing freely through your being to create your life experience, you feel blissful.

This is the simple message of this material. If you actually experience what is presented in this book and CD, you will increase your fulfillment in life. Guaranteed.

To begin studying this Modern Spirituality manual, ask yourself one all-important question and answer honestly: "How happy am I from day to day?" Take a moment to ask yourself that question and pause to sense what arises in reply. Are you actually content? Do you like yourself, even love yourself? How are your relationships, your health, your career? What fills the moments of each day -- joy or anxiety? How happy are you from day to day?

Experience Comes First

Before we continue, pause for a moment and focus your attention. Slow your reading... in fact, pause between words for a moment. Become aware of your breathing. Notice your expanding awareness... and how that is changing the way you feel. Experience yourself being present... fully present in this here and now moment.

Now, return to normal reading. That is how easy it is to experience Source. It is here, always here, hidden in plain sight! But most of the time we are unconsciously careening between one external experience and another, with our busy minds tossing out random thoughts and our emotions swirling in a turmoil of feelings.

No wonder meditation feels good! It's a relief to get away from all that chaos. But that's not really the primary purpose of meditation. Meditation, which I advocate as the first essential practice for expanding your experience of fulfillment in life, is meant to balance your internal and external experience. Other than sleeping, most people are obsessed with external activities all day long. This is stressful and imbalanced. When you meditate, even for just a few minutes, you increase the ratio of your internal-to-external experience, which is a small step towards restoring balance. It's a type of balance you have rarely experienced with any consistency in our busy, externally-focused world of the West.

It feels good to be balanced. There is a comfort and confidence that develops from standing on solid ground. But meditation is also training for the conscious mind. Instead of allowing your thoughts to live their own life, you begin to direct them, perhaps with a mantra or an affirmation; you learn how to be in the witness space of "no thought." I will provide more detail on this later, but it's important to emphasize here at the beginning that it is impossible to experience the fullness of life – which is really known through the heart - without having a disciplined, conscious mind.

Consciousness... It's Where We Live

Regardless of where we reside and what we do, the truth is that all of us experience life within the context of our consciousness. Yes, we have an individual consciousness, but it is not separate from universal consciousness. Consciousness is one. True fulfillment comes as we learn to live where individual and universal consciousness merge.

While many modern texts present life as a duality and give examples like light and dark, action and inaction, etc., the ancient Vedic and Tantric texts (which were born over 8,000 years ago from the revelations of great sages) all taught that creation is a trinity. Yes, there are those two balancing polarities, but in-between them is a space. This is home. This is where we all belong, present in this space between the two polarities. As it is, most people live in their external, activity-laden environment. They may seek solace in meditation or sleep, but it becomes an either-or choice because they do not understand how to become fully present in balance between the two polarities.

As you study the following materials, listen to the High-Tech Meditation CD, and learn how to occupy that space between those two polarities. You will balance your human system and gradually condition your body, mind, and emotions to naturally seek this balance point, rather than unconsciously pursue addictive imbalances. Your moments will be increasingly filled with the innate joy of being, instead of struggles to give up what you think is "bad" for you. You will increasingly experience that being human is a blissful experience in and of itself. You will notice yourself becoming happy for no particular reason, other than that you are alive.

The Five-Fold Learning Process

This book and enclosed CD represent an introductory course of study. I'm sure that you have had a great variety of learning experiences during your lifetime, some more successful than others. Ultimately, what matters is being able to integrate what you learn. How many times have you enjoyed a peak experience of some kind, say in a seminar, only to lose what you seemed to gain a few days after returning to work? To eliminate this problem, I teach all my students a five-fold learning process.

1. The peak experience comes first and is often highly enjoyable. Whenever you experience something profound, endorphins flood your body and that feels good! But any peak experience that isn't integrated can quickly fade. The "high" should lead to an actual evolutionary advance, which is a distinct, second step.

2. Evolution. You notice that something has changed, that you are somehow more than you were before. Your self-

awareness has expanded, your consciousness has evolved, you feel different.

3. The third learning step is illumination and this represents a further expansion of self-awareness. Now, creative insights arise relative to the peak experience. To whatever degree these insights are an upgrade beyond your existing data, processing is now required.

4. Processing a peak experience is similar to upgrading the software on your computer. This fourth step is where many earnest students have trouble, understandably, because so little guidance is provided. It seems more exciting to just camp out where the peak experiences are and grab for one after another. Inevitably, however, the peak sensation subsides. Now those wonderful insights slam headlong into past experience. Perhaps you've returned to work and there it is, the same situation you left just a few hours or days before. Processing is required to install the new programs and uninstall the old ones. That takes some understanding, the development of specific skills, and intelligent guidance.

5. The final learning step is integration. Integration occurs through repeating the new behaviors connected to what you've learned. That is best done in a daily personal practice, which you will learn about in a later chapter on the Holistic Lifestyle.

Balance

The primary principle in the Holistic Model and the Holistic

Lifestyle is balance. You will be learning how to balance your physical, mental and emotional experience throughout the day with a variety of techniques, all emerging from the simple principle of being present in the here and now space. I refer to these as the "Technologies of Now."

Ultimately, you can learn to embrace balance as your primary objective in any moment. But until you have experienced this five-fold learning process and the fulfillment that it brings, the immediate promise of peak experiences will tend to seduce you. Obviously, the pay-off is instant. But, over the long-term, integrated, evolutionary experience is far more fulfilling. Again, it will be the actual experience that will win you over, not any words that I can speak or write.

The Play of Consciousness

I mentioned that all of us share the same context, namely that we live within our consciousness. I also emphasized that consciousness is one and whole. One way to picture this is to consider the ocean with its waves. The ocean is unified. Deep beneath the surface, all is dark and there is virtually no movement. Yet, as we move toward the surface, the same ocean begins to show signs of activity, light, and flow. Up on the surface, waves move with an infinite diversity, each wave unique to itself. Although no wave is exactly the same as any other, all are connected within the unity of the ocean. Each wave is an individual expression of the wholeness of the ocean; the ocean and its waves are the same one.

Consciousness is the ocean and we are the waves. We are all

one in that wholeness and individual within ourselves, and we are all connected with each other. What is the ultimate purpose of this consciousness that we share? Here in the West there is an obsession with meaning, so all sorts of meanings are ascribed to life. In truth, the purpose of consciousness is to experience itself! It's that simple. Consciousness was created in order to know itself. Fully. In fact, all experience in consciousness is meant for its own entertainment. Does that sound frivolous? It's what all the ancient texts taught, that there really is nothing serious going on here! Consciousness is entertained by its creation and it delights in the process. Remember, its innate nature is bliss. Joy. Happiness.

At the highest level of truthful unified consciousness, life is a joke. If you don't believe me, look around. Honestly, does any of this make much sense? In fact, our world seems increasingly like an insane asylum where the inmates have locked themselves up and lost the key. Of course, any one of us can free ourselves at any time to reclaim a joyful experience, a sane experience, by plugging back into Source and choosing to live in balance. And, because we are all connected in the oneness of consciousness, we instantly affect each other.

In The Beginning

The ancient texts teach that out of the Great Mystery, referred to in Buddhism as the Void (or the Pregnant Void), this universe of seeming duality, formlessness and form emerged. Scientists teach that a Big Bang started it all. The Sanskrit word for this is "*spanda*," a moment back in time when this reality we inhabit first manifested. This was the origin of "relative" reality, that is, a seeming duality: formlessness and form, being and becoming, anti-matter and matter, etc.

Well, what caused this Big Bang? The intention in consciousness. The primary intention was for consciousness to fully be itself, know itself, and experience itself. Therefore, consciousness created this relative field which is where we are right now, as a place for all experience to occur. In Sanskrit, this is referred to as *Chitshakti Vilas*, the play of consciousness.

Releasing Judgment

Any experience you are having is the play of consciousness of the moment, the experience whose time has come. It is perfectly appropriate relative to your own evolution. Imagine, actually having that understanding and the experience of unconditional acceptance in every circumstance! Well, you can. In fact, it's natural. It's what you are growing into. How can I be so sure of that? Well, you're reading this book. You have an interest in these things. If you didn't, you wouldn't be reading this right now; you would be doing something else. And that would be perfectly appropriate as well.

But, since you're here, we know that you are interested in conscious evolution, and I am delighted to offer my guidance. Understand, guidance of some kind is absolutely necessary. Why? Because the journey you are undertaking is fraught with challenges. In fact, your reality begins changing. Of course, I know it already has.

I also know that your identity has been shifting. It will continue to do so. Yes, it can be uncomfortable, to be neither this nor that, in between where you were and will be, who you were and who you will be in conscious experience. Relax. You couldn't possibly be more on schedule if you tried. While you're at it, also let go of your hope for "enlightenment". Rather, embrace the enlightening experience that is happening now, now and always now.

Because you do not understand everything that is happening to you in this evolutionary process in your consciousness (how could you, your mechanisms for understanding are still growing), you will tend to judge certain experiences that you have as being "wrong". "This shouldn't be happening to me!" Yes it should! It is a result. It is what is appropriate to your learning. But it takes something to see it that way. They say that "when the student is ready, the teacher appears". But the teacher is not just someone like me. Your teacher is each moment of your experience. What is presented to you is always, always for your learning and ongoing evolution. This includes the partner you thought was supposed to make you happy and the career that was supposed to fulfill you. Sorry! That is not their real purpose. Everything is here to help you expand and grow into the fullness of who you already are in essence. That is why it is so important to learn to pay attention to what is actually happening, so you can leverage your lessons all the way from peak through integration.

Opening to Source

Are you plugged in? Can you open to the possibility of Source, universal consciousness, God-by-whatever-name having a relationship with you? This is profoundly different from developing a relationship with a theoretical God that you create in your own image. This is about surrendering into relationship with the eternal source of all, present here and now and not separate from you at all. When you are able to embrace this reality and experience Source Consciousness -- not as a distant concept but as the true nature of reality -- you experience yourself, the truth of who you are and what life is, in this eternal present moment.

That is fulfillment.

If you want to get a suntan, bask in the sun. Similarly, if you want to have an enlightening experience, place yourself close to a source of enlightening energy. So... right here and right now... in this very moment... relax into the frequency of enlightening joy... This is your true nature... and this is where I live. I hope we have the opportunity to meet one day and that we find ourselves resonating together in this unified frequency that I have experienced over many years as "home." It is just as much your home as it is mine, even though I may have been living here a little longer than you have. It cannot be owned because it already belongs to us all in the oneness of consciousness. This space, it turns out, is who "I am."

Being here, now, together, is fulfillment.

ॐ

Part Two

Stories of Fulfillment

Part Two
Stories of Fulfillment

Over the years, those who have been drawn to study Modern Spirituality have often experienced dramatic and ongoing personal transformation. Yes, there are epiphanies to be enjoyed, momentary peak experiences that might be remembered as turning points, but these are always preceded by some sort of effort and followed by an ongoing practice that integrates them.

This is not good news in our instant gratification culture where fulfillment is promised with a click of the remote, but it **is** the way it is. Anyone who has achieved an extraordinary level of lasting success and achievement in some area of their lives will tell you that it didn't happen in an instant. I've heard celebrities joke that they worked hard for thirty years to become an overnight sensation.

Mona was a well-established and successful psychotherapist who sensed that something was missing in her life. "I endured a persistent, underlying emptiness and dissatisfaction. But High-Tech Meditation helped me to finally address this. I now feel a deep connection beyond myself, within myself. The sense of lack has transformed into a feeling of wholeness and I often laugh to myself, simply because being alive has become so fulfilling!"

Mona wasn't really stuck; she was steadily evolving towards conscious contact with exactly what she needed to take her experience to the next level. Because she is a professional "helper," she has now been able to pass her personal gains along to associates, being a more effective therapist who is genuinely walking her talk.

Dave is a university administrator who has worked in a hostile environment for a good part of his career. "University faculty often view and treat senior administrators with contempt, and tension generally pervades our meetings. But, after several years of High-Tech Meditation, I found myself experiencing an expanding sense of mental stillness plus a growth of compassion and empathy for my colleagues. As this inner transformation occurred, I noticed that my outer world seemed to become more friendly and supportive.

"This phenomenon was most apparent when one faculty member who had been particularly confrontational for years thanked me for all that I do for him and the rest of the faculty. It was an amazing moment. I also noticed that my daily interaction with other faculty members had become much more cordial. I had to acknowledge that these outer changes were occurring as a result of my inner transformation.

"I have proven that, as I cultivate an improved personal state of being, I become more productive and successful, and with much less effort. Further, I am becoming less focused on results and more content with my moment-to-moment flow of existence. Ironically, even though the past couple of years have been difficult for many institutions due to economic constraints, my own institutional budget has continued to increase significantly. Evidently, paying attention to 'being' makes the 'doing more effective and with less effort!"

Dave demonstrated how the power of *inner* change reflects as *outer* change in his immediate environment. I appreciate his comments about how "what happened" did not require much effort. His experience can inspire us all to take the easy way - not to be lazy, but to actualize an internal practice.

Helen used to be a worrier, highly strung, nervous, pessimistic and depressed, with low self-esteem and she was unhappy most of time. "I questioned the meaning and purpose of life and my place within it. I blamed others and circumstances for my state of mind and emotion and I played the victim role expertly. This was not a satisfying existence!

"Meditation flipped the switch from darkness to light and totally turned my life around. My family will tell you how much I've transformed... 'changed' isn't a strong-enough term. Through meditation I discovered the truth of who I am and what life is about. This is a gift I wish for everybody."

It's fascinating how the simple act of closing your eyes and stilling the mind can accomplish so much transformative good! High-Tech Meditation conditions brain-function so that it makes sense that there **would** be a reflection throughout all aspects of your life. After all, you take your brain with you wherever you go!

Bob found that as he deepened his personal practice he was challenged to face his fears, accept his failures and learn how to become inclusive, rather than exclusive, which had been a long-standing personal habit. "I really had to relinquish my egoic preferences and that was painful. But it was worth it. Relationships with family and friends have become more intimate and gentle. My body has lost many of its aches and pains. I witness my mind with ever more amusement, as its hold over me loses power. Life is much simpler now, with fewer 'wants' and more appreciation for my riches."

What Bob is sharing emphasizes how this kind of deep meditative work is not a cake-walk. Whatever information is present in a person's database that does not resonate with the new frequencies they are evolving to embody – such as habits of thinking, beliefs and prejudices, behaviors and habits – will arise to be upgraded. This calls for the kind of truth-telling Bob did, being honest with himself and remaining true to the evolved self he experienced himself becoming.

Deborah struggled with anxiety and depression and had been taking medications for ten years. "I started the Recognitions High-Tech Meditation program in 2005 and began applying Synchronicity tools. Incredibly, not only was my need for the meds completely eliminated over time, but my entire state of being transformed. My family was amazed. I am now enjoying an experience that my heart had always yearned for but never truly believed was possible. This opportunity for radical evolution is a precious and desperately needed gift in the world!"

Anyone on medication for a medical condition needs to exercise care when they change aspects of their lifestyle. It's always wise to let your doctor know what you are doing and have him or her track your body's changing needs for medication. In many cases that need will lessen as balance is re-established and the system returns to working order.

Bonnie is a massage therapist and teaches massage. "Regular meditation has added great insights and effectiveness to my healing ability and teaching skills. Clients and students have noticed and commented on my increased focus, insights, and creativity over the last few years. Some call it charisma, others just say they like being in my healing presence. I find this amazing... and I am very honored to be able to share it. It's meditation that has brought balance into my life, brought me into the here-and-now moment. I love being able to access all the subtle dimensions that are a part of me."

People do notice the changes. Some are thrilled; others might feel challenged. It depends on their own state of consciousness and the direction in which they are moving themselves. Anyone who has embraced their evolutionary journey will appreciate a friend who is deepening their own conscious practice as a leader showing them the way. For others less primed for transformation, your positive personal change might seem like an imposition of threatening beliefs and behaviors, without your saying a word. They feel the energy, which invites a depth of change they are simply not ready to make. This can be especially challenging when it happens with family members. How important it is to remember that everyone is exactly where their feet are, having the experience they are meant to have! There is no judgment, of oneself or of anyone else. All of us are on schedule!

Caroline lives in our Virginia Synchronicity Sanctuary. She described how she has changed since she began her association. "I have let go of what I had previously taken as reality and entered into the unknown. It is filled with creativity, infinite possibilities and a knowing based on the wisdom of my own conscious choices as the creator of my reality. The peace and joy that I have experienced through 'unlearning' all that I thought I knew before is so very valuable.

"This has increased my personal power, not by efforting or through goal orientation, not by getting anything external to myself, but through my daily meditation practice, through truthful understanding, and by consistently living the holistic model of reality."

Unlearning, or deprogramming, is an important step in the process of tapping into universal wisdom for oneself. Those who taught us – parents, teachers, mentors and friends - did the best they could, but they were entrained to those who taught them and inevitably passed along that dysfunction to us. Consider who your teachers were. How attuned were they to a truthful experience of reality? What were their values, what did they emphasize in their communication with you? All of that, all that you "learned," becomes challenged when you commit to a precision meditative practice. It takes time and consistent attention to disrupt those ingrained patterns, which is why a daily practice is required.

Sook Yin is a physician who has learned to deal with problems more effectively. "I recently ordered a large quantity of nutritional supplements from abroad. In my enthusiasm to try this new product, I forgot to check if the formulation adhered to local guidelines. After an unusually long delay, I was notified that the consignment had been held back because one of the products exceeded the permissible dose and was not allowed into the country. It took innumerable phone calls to come up with a solution, but I noticed that the way I handled this was remarkably different than before. I remained calm and did not get angry or frustrated at all. I know this was a result of my work with High-Tech Meditation and the Synchronicity materials. I am now able to see problems in perspective and deal with them in a more detached manner."

Problems like Sook Yin's are unavoidable. Life happens to all of us and it's seldom exactly the way we would prefer it to be. How we handle our challenges is the question. Sook Yin discovered that she was more able to stay on top of this situation and deal with it in a centered way. How valuable this is, and how essential, because we can be sure that there are more and larger challenges ahead for all of us. Preparing now, before crises strike, makes good sense.

One of our Synchronicity associates is a creative artist with an insatiable desire for the truth. Soon after she started meditating she began to notice how the stories she was telling herself allowed her to stay anchored in illusion. "This awareness led to discovering why I created those stories in the first place and that began a magnificent unraveling. Eventually, the truth of myself became the vision I now hold, because all the unwelcome baggage had just dropped away."

Who would you be without your stories? Most of us define ourselves through our stories about what's happened to us. We live in the past, identified with a person that these things happened to. This is not exactly creating our own reality. It is laboring in illusion! Becoming aware of this fact is an important first step. Next, we can let this "unraveling" begin, so that an authentic experience of self and life can emerge. Imagine... in fact, ask yourself: "Who would I be, without my stories?"

Jim experienced a dramatic spiritual awakening in 1977 when he read The *Only Dance There Is* by Ram Dass. "This book evoked an internal response in me that I can only call 'resonance.' This was what I had been waiting for. I had known there was something missing in my life, but I'd had no clue as to what it might actually be until I read that book. I began meditating regularly and immediately discovered what had been missing: meditation! Meditation became my primary interest in life.

I had many enlightening moments during the next sixteen years, but I didn't have any personal guidance and that finally burned me out so I took a ten-year hiatus from the pursuit of freedom and enlightenment.

In 1993 I regained my hunger for meditation and found a sample tape from Synchronicity. It seems that I had ordered the tape seven or eight years before but never actually listened to it. Now was the time. The moment I listened to the tape I knew that this was for me. It delivered the best meditation I had ever had! Of course, I immediately called and ordered the Recognitions Program. My experience of life quickly shifted and everything began to lose its seriousness. Now I find myself enjoying life more and more each day and I can say with all honesty that I am truly fulfilled!"

When the student is ready, the teacher appears. Jim was right on schedule every step of the way, just as you are reading this book right now. It's habitual to judge ourselves and make our history wrong, but I encourage you to embrace the steps that brought you to this moment. What's more important is where you go from here. A book is just a book. A CD is just a CD. What you choose to do with them is what will determine how much of a difference this makes in your life.

I chose to include these personal accounts from a few of our associates because they communicate real experiences. Each person has written about how they have applied the principles you are now studying towards personal challenges in their lives. Practicing from day to day – rather than just understanding in our heads – is what creates lasting change.

Our foundation is set now, with basic principles articulated and real life examples of application provided. In the next section, we emphasize the most important tool for creating balance in your life: meditation. Many of you will have had experience with meditation already. I invite you to suspend your beliefs about it and open your awareness to learn of a very different modern meditative experience: High-Tech Meditation. And, for those of you who have never meditated, welcome to a new world of inner exploration.

ॐ

Part Three

High-Tech Meditation

Part Three
High-Tech Meditation

Daily meditation is your primary balancing practice. If you are not currently meditating, you can begin now, using the sample High-Tech Meditation CD that accompanies this book. If you are already meditating regularly, using the CD when you meditate will introduce you to the difference that precision High-Tech Meditation makes. There are three reasons why daily meditation is so important.

1. It's a practice. You're doing something, not just wishing your life was better. Our systems respond to action of any kind, especially when we start an activity we believe will benefit us. This means that as you begin meditating - or shift your practice to High-Tech Meditation and stick with it - you will automatically begin to feel better about yourself.

2. Regular meditation develops the frontal lobes of your brain.

3. Regular meditation helps develop witness consciousness, strengthens the "muscle" of self-awareness and enhances personal holistic power.

Why is that important? The frontal lobes are your CEO, the seat of attention and concentration, what you use to make critical judgments for organization and planning. It's what separates humans from animals, and it also plays a role in how happy you feel.

A Wisconsin study of stressed-out technology sector workers conducted through the University of Massachusetts Medical School, over an eight-week period, regularly measured participants' brain-wave activity. The results indicated a profound shift towards the left frontal lobe in the meditators and these individuals reported feeling significantly calmer and happier than the control group who did not meditate.

When you commit to a daily meditation practice, you will expand your brain capacity and develop skills that are vital for a fulfilled life. It's simply one of the best investments any person can make.

The Problem with Meditation

Meditation is an ancient practice, originating over 7,000 years ago. Today's world is immeasurably more complex and, while modern technology has yielded many benefits, it has also created a vast network of energies - from the electrical wiring in our homes and offices, to the TV, radio and microwaves that bombard us 24 hours a day, and the ever-increasing pollution that lowers our oxygen levels. Consider also the exploding world population, wars and starvation, stress and conflict in traffic-clogged cities, court rooms charged with animosity, government gridlocks, relationships on tilt ... it goes on and on. These are truly unprecedented times in terms of environmental and energetic stressors. Additionally, most beginning meditators – and even some veterans - fight with their minds, constantly assailed by random thoughts and feelings of impatience or irritation.

Of course, it helps to do everything you can to create a quiet, distraction-free environment, but that is virtually impossible to do these days. How can you shut out the electrical frequencies, the wireless signals, etc? You can't. And how do you quiet those thoughts, especially when "time is money" and moments spent in meditative silence can seem totally "unproductive," especially in an increasingly desperate economy? These problems are real. They show up day after day. And they explain why the Synchronicity Foundation for Modern Spirituality has invested the last thirty years in developing and refining High-Tech Meditation.

High-Tech Meditation

The CD that accompanies this book is a sample of the High-Tech Meditation proprietary technology that thousands of Synchronicity associates around the world have utilized for decades. According to the research conducted by Cade and Coxhead, the use of sonic entrainment technology successfully overrides environmental interference and decelerates brain-wave patterns.[1] As brain-waves (beta, alpha, theta, and delta) decelerate, whole-brain synchrony or hemispheric balance proportionally increases and generates a peaceful balance in the brain, the experience of "wholeness."

High-Tech Meditation has been proven to create whole-brain synchrony four times faster than traditional, non-technological forms of meditation. It is highly pleasurable and becomes an activity you will look forward to, rather than something that's supposed to be good for you that you really can't wait to finish.

All Synchronicity High-Tech Meditation soundtracks deliver easy access to states of holistic awareness traditionally achieved only after many years of disciplined practice. Each soundtrack may be used alone or in conjunction with any other meditative techniques you may presently practice. You can begin listening to the enclosed CD at any time, even though this slim volume is designed to give you the conceptual framework to really understand how High-Tech Meditation works.

A Choice for Life

How are you living your life? Many people focus almost completely on manipulating their outside environment. Others grow their consciousness and learn how to create from the inside out. High-Tech meditation is for these individuals and you must be one of them, because you are reading this book!

The quiet moments you spend alone each day meditating will become an increasingly productive part of your life. And now you can utilize High-Tech Meditation to develop whole-brain synchrony and accelerate the expansion of your holistic awareness. The resulting increased internal balance will begin to reflect externally, as you learn how to practice the Holistic Lifestyle and experience your own holistic reality – a developed skill, not just a compelling theory.

☙

Part Four

The Recognitions Program

Part Four
The Recognitions Program

The Recognitions Program is much more than a meditation program. It is designed for those committed individuals whose intention is to actualize and integrate wholeness in their daily life experience. It works on both the interior (subjective) and the exterior (objective) levels and it supports the development of the Holistic Lifestyle.

The Holistic Lifestyle is a fundamentally different way of living, where fulfillment is experienced through "being," not "doing." While we've all heard that happiness comes from the inside, just hearing those words (and perhaps believing them) doesn't make them so. How **does** a person actually become happy, and stay happy, from the inside rather than requiring it from outside stimulation? It's a remarkable experience that develops through living in balance, rather than depending on imbalanced excesses for peak experiences of enjoyment.

Modern day culture actually programs us to rely on addictive substances, vicarious thrills through celebrities, and extreme activities to produce happiness. Such experiences are fleeting. Sustained happiness is very different. It is only available by living in balance - physically, emotionally and mentally. This is known as a pleasurable state of internal "rest," and is available for every person who learns how to actualize it. This state is described in the Bible as "the secret place of the most high."[1] The Bhagavad Gita promises, "When meditation is mastered, the mind is unwavering like the flame of a lamp in a windless place."[2] This is the state of being that the Holistic Lifestyle develops and the Recognitions Program is our primary tool for growing that ability, when used on a daily basis.

I created Recognitions in 1983 and have continually refined and updated it over these past almost-thirty years. It is a transformational audio program supported with personal mentoring. Recognitions utilizes Synchronicity Holodynamic Vibrational Entrainment Technology (HVET), also known as Synchronicity Sonic Technology, to decelerate brain-wave frequencies. This increases balance and holistic awareness.

Brainwave Frequencies

The Synchronicity research team uses our own "Brain Monitor" to measure Beta, Alpha, Theta and Delta frequency ranges in our meditators. We have determined that regular use of Synchronicity High-Tech Meditation technology through the Recognitions Program decelerates brain-wave activities from Alpha through Delta, enhancing a range of experience from light relaxation to deep transcendental meditation.

Beta brain-waves are the fastest, vibrating in the 12 – 38 Hz. range. Associated with left-brain, logic-oriented, linear thinking, they support us for problem-solving and focus. But too much Beta activity indicates stress and anxiety, which is what most people experience most of the time.

Synchronicity High-Tech Meditation practiced through the

Recognitions Program decelerates brain wave activity, slowing from Beta to Alpha, which operates in the 8 – 13 Hz. range. When your brain is producing Alpha frequencies, you experience a pleasant, comfortable, mildly relaxed yet wakeful state of awareness. This is a welcome relief for those struggling with a stress-filled lifestyle and is the first stage of meditation.

Theta brain-waves in the 3.5 – 7 Hz. range produce a blissful sense of well-being similar to Alpha and also expand a state of holistic awareness where creativity and imagery predominate. Experienced meditators are accustomed to a wide variety of "inner" images and visions, which seem to correlate with increased Theta activity.

Delta brain waves are the slowest, 0 – 3.5 Hz. and are traditionally associated with deep sleep. Only the most advanced meditators can remain conscious while producing Delta brain-waves.

Comparative Studies

Novices (those meditating five years or less) have been tested and found to consistently produce mid to high-frequency Alpha waves. Moderately experienced meditators (ten to twenty years) produced low frequency Alpha, with the frequency decreasing with increasing experience. Veteran meditators (twenty to forty years experience) produced Theta frequencies in the 5 – 6 Hz. range.

Our extensive research on Recognitions meditators indicates that most begin with an ability to produce Alpha at 11 or 12 Hz, consistent with the "novice" level. Over time, their brain-wave patterns shift with the Alpha peaks becoming lower in frequency, larger in amplitude, and more persistent over time. As they acquire more experience, Theta and even Delta develop. Our Brain Monitor scans confirm that test subjects (none with more than seven years of meditation experience in the Recognitions Program) produce brain-wave patterns consistent with those generated by Buddhist monks who have been meditating twenty years or more. Our results indicate Recognitions can produce a four-fold acceleration factor over classical methods of meditation.

Monthly Recognitions Facilitation

The Recognitions Program includes audio CD's plus monthly phone calls and email coaching with a trained facilitator. Recognitions Facilitators have many years of experience practicing Synchronicity High-Tech Meditation and living the Holistic Lifestyle. These monthly dialogues validate changing experience in ways not possible on one's own. Questions are welcomed and specific guidance is provided with a "theme" for each month. As the meditative experience deepens and personal clarity increases, participants tend to find positive changes developing in all aspects of their lives.

The enclosed CD provides an opportunity to sample Synchronicity High-Tech Meditation. Those interested in more information about the Recognitions Program can visit www.synchronicity.org/recognitions or call 1-800-962-2033 or 434-361-2323.

࿇

Part Five

The Holistic Lifestyle

Part Five
The Holistic Lifestyle

It's one thing to contemplate how to create a fulfilling life; it's another thing to actually enjoy it consistently. The purpose of Synchronicity Foundation for Modern Spirituality is to support those who are ready and willing to do exactly that. While life is and always will be fundamentally mysterious, there is actually no mystery to creating the fulfilling life that everyone intuits is somehow possible.

In his 1937 book, *Think and Grow Rich*, Napoleon Hill focused on controlling thoughts to achieve success. He mentioned thoughts themselves and also the energy in thoughts that attract other thoughts. Hill chose to refer to his "secret"[1] only indirectly (about a hundred times within the book, he said), but the 2006 film, *The Secret*, spelled it out. It's the Law of Attraction: "…your thoughts and your feelings create your life."[2]

True as that principle may be, what's inadequately explained in Western interpretations of ancient texts is the energy factor. Creating your fulfilled life requires focusing personal power through your thoughts and feelings. The important question then is: what is the quality and quantity of your personal power? That's what really determines your success in creating a fulfilled life from the inside out.

The best way for any person to increase and refine the quality of their personal power is not by reading books, having regular revelations, or even studying with a Master. It comes through practicing what is known as the Holistic Lifestyle. Yes, it's a practice, something you do every day. That's the only way to achieve the results you seek. In fact, "it" only becomes a reality by living it, never by merely seeking it.

The Five Principles of Holistic Living

Every structure that is built to survive any length of time must have a strong foundation. Before we consider how you will practice the Holistic Lifestyle, it's important to establish the foundational understanding it rests upon. In this case, there are five principles that affirm your sovereignty as the creator of your life experience, in oneness with Source. These are worded in the first person because they describe what is true for you and every human being. As such, they may be used as affirmations of presently existing truth.

Principle One: I am Source, I am the Power.

There is only One. One Source Consciousness is the essence of all. Source is all, empowers all, and manifests as all, including every human being. Therefore, in oneness, I am Source, I am the Power.

Principle Two: I create my creation.

One Source Consciousness creates the creation and creation cannot be different from the creator. There is only One. I am Source. All is Source. Therefore, as Source, I create my creation.

Principle Three: I am responsible for my creation.

One Source Consciousness creates the creation, which is itself. Source is responsible for its creation because there is no "other." I am Source, therefore I am responsible for my creation.

Principle Four: I can change my creation.

The creation is the play of the creator constantly diversifying the experience of itself. As Source, I am constantly diversifying the experience of myself.

Principle Five: I am one and I am free.

One Source Consciousness is all. There is nothing beyond it or additional to it. It is independent and free. As Source, I am One, independent and free.

Balance

The Holistic Lifestyle develops from the Holistic Model, which orients around one primary principle: balance. The Holistic Lifestyle involves living at the balance point. When this familiar world of ours emerged from Source, it differentiated into the two polarities of relative reality... light and dark, stillness and action, being and becoming, etc. Between these two polarities is a balance point, a space without which neither could exist.

Without that space between them, they would be one and that would be the end of relative reality! What is that space? It is the place of balance where holistic awareness, or "witness" consciousness resides. Also known as "the eternal now," it is where you experience the balance of these two polarities. It must be an experience, known in the here and now. In other words, holistic awareness becomes known as your actual experience of now. Your first tactile experience of this space may come during meditation and could be described as "detached observation." You discover that you are watching yourself. But you are not yet watching yourself <u>as the same consciousness</u>. You are still separate, watching as something separate from that which is watched. As holistic experience evolves, individuated witness consciousness progresses into unified witness consciousness. Watcher and the watched are the same One, in truth, and that becomes the truthful experience for anyone who persists with their balancing practice.

This eternal "now" of holistic awareness is associated with the heart-field, the center of individuated consciousness. The heart-field is the gateway to holistic awareness, but few people can easily access the heart-field because the mind-field interferes. Busy thoughts get in the way. This is one reason why meditation is prescribed, to quiet (or balance) the mind-field so that it can be transcended. Then the heart-field can be accessed, which is what opens holistic awareness within the eternal now. You feel it, you don't just think it. It's an experience, not a theory.

Note that there is no final "enlightenment" to aim for or arrive at. The word itself is a misnomer because the process of expanding wholeness is an eternal dynamic. It had no beginning and there will be no end. What a relief! No final goal, just the delighting progression of ever more enlightening, holistic experience.

The Trinity of Human Experience
Most of us are dominantly aware of our physical, emotional, and mental levels of experience. These are the densest but not the

only levels of consciousness. There are subtler dimensions as well and, when they interact with the dense dimensions, we can begin to experience what it truly means to be a whole human being.

The connection between subtle and dense dimensions occurs in this balance point that we have been speaking of. The balance point is always right now and right here amidst the experience that is actually happening. Contemplate that for a moment, because it is typical to believe that deep, meaningful experiences must arise from special circumstances. Not so. It may be that certain circumstances support the merging of the dense and subtle, but that is because they assist us to be fully present. Even meditation is a practice that trains us to stay put, long after the meditation period ends.

I challenge my mentoring students to observe how long they can maintain a balanced state throughout their day. When do they "lose it?" Is it the traffic jam en route to work, an argument with a spouse or friend, an irritating phone call, something on the news, or their own out-of-control thoughts or feelings? I teach them to watch and learn. What is the distraction? Of course, that's the moment to balance, to focus on this space between the polarities, rather than getting sucked into the excessive or obsessive experience of any extreme. As it says in the Bhagavad Gita, "In joy not overjoyed, in sorrow not dejected."[3] The state of balance itself is what delivers the most holistic fulfillment, because wholeness is proportional to balance.

The problem is there is usually an immediate pay-off to imbalance. For instance, the sugar rush, the forbidden sexual encounter, the adrenaline blast of beating an opponent. Imbalance seems to feel so good, at least for a while. How can balance feel even better? Until it does, temptation will always win. Let's create a balancing experience right now and see how it feels. Slow down your reading. Focus your attention on each word as you read it, without trying to gain meaning or finish the line or paragraph quickly. Feel your relationship with these words, the intimacy of pausing in the spaces between the words. Drop your agenda. Release your hopes for finding fulfillment in this book. Just read. And be with yourself having the experience of reading. Let your attention touching on each word be enough. Witness yourself reading. And become aware of the subtle peace that permeates this here-and-now moment.

If you are able to slow down and generate this experience, it gives you a sense of the subtler dimensions which I am referring to. Savor your momentary experience right now, whatever it may be. Welcome this world of heightened, subtle awareness that has opened. And know that this and much, much more is possible in every circumstance. In fact, it is meant to become a way of living, the Holistic Lifestyle. It is achievable, one moment at a time, and in every conceivable circumstance. This is a fulfillment that you *bring* into your dimensional experience, not extract from it.

The Five Truths of the Holistic Model

The Five Principles of Holistic Living are applied in your life through what we term the Holistic Lifestyle, introduced in the next Section. These principles flow through five truths:

1. **There is only One.** That One is the essence, by whatever

name. We can call it Source, Consciousness, God, Life, etc. By whatever name, there is only One. This One creates relative reality.

2. **Relative reality is the arena of all experience.** This requires the illusion of separation as the primary illusion in consciousness, and the ego as the instrument for the illusory separation in consciousness.

3. **The heart-field is the gateway to the experience of the eternal now.** All holistic models of reality describe the heart-field as the gateway of the "now" of consciousness. The only true experience of reality is in the "here and now."

4. **The mind-field dominates for most people.** The ego-driven mind-field dominates the heart-field with the illusion of separation. This results in the forfeiture of holistic awareness. Therefore, the first learning priority must be to balance the mind-field.

5. **Balance increases as the mind-field is transcended.** The egocentric experience of illusion must be transcended through balance, so that the heart-field can be accessed. The heart-field is the gateway. This opens the experience of truthful reality within the eternal "now."

Your Real Life – A Play in Consciousness

How entertaining is your life? Maybe it's a tragedy at times. Well, that can be entertaining. Some people go to the theater to watch thrillers and even enjoy being scared. Next time, it might be a comedy, which could also be enjoyable.

Life is like an ever-changing movie. If you can witness it, rather than jumping up on the stage to try and change it, then the process itself becomes enjoyable. It's not so much the content – which is always changing – as it is the act of witnessing. That's another way of talking about being aware, "holistic" awareness. Holistic awareness arises from the balance point between polarities and is enjoyable in itself. We have all had this experience already, frequently, although we may not remember it this way.

As babies, we were simply aware, albeit in very limited ways. Yes, we cried when we were hungry or tired. Our needs were simple and we wanted them filled immediately! But, think about what you see in a baby's eyes … curiosity, fascination, interest. Without a judging mind yet developed, the baby is simply aware.

Your real life is a play in consciousness, always entertaining, as opposed to your artificial life, which is the processed version happening between your ears. To be holistically aware and enjoy your life requires what is sometimes called "beginner's mind," which really means grabbing the reins of your mind (which is usually spewing out life-negative and fear-based manipulations) and directing truthful, life-affirmative and love-based thoughts. This is a skill that will take time to develop, but it starts with awareness. You become aware that your mind is interfering with your enjoyment of the show. If you were in a theater, you'd tell someone in front of you to sit down so you could see. Similarly, you tell your fragmented mind to be still when it is blathering on about how terrible everything is, especially how "inadequate" you are.

Practical Steps to an Enlightening Experience

Truly wise teachers always point to the here and now as the best (only) time and place to enjoy enlightening experience. They are not talking about theories and neither am I. We all speak of paying attention, such as listening to the melody of the stream, feeling the wind, hearing the birds, enjoying the flowers in blossom. This is not symbolic. We are talking about actually becoming aware of what is happening in the moment. This requires freeing yourself from self-talk and emotional overload.

The Holistic Lifestyle focuses on bringing balance to your physical, emotional and mental experience. Why do we focus here, rather than on more esoteric levels? Because the real world of these three dimensions provides our connecting points to higher levels of awareness.

If you have ever played a piano, you will understand that every note appears in several octaves. When you strike "C" in a low octave, it resonates with the "C" in a higher octave. It has produced what is called a "harmonic." This is true for every note in every octave. Similarly, when your physical dimension is balanced, that frequency resonates with a harmonic at a higher, invisible level. Likewise with the mental and emotional dimensions.

This is why we start here, balancing these dimensions. This is what gives us access to those higher realms. To go after higher realms directly, while ignoring these three basic dimensions, is just a head trip, regardless of the spiritual words that might be used to describe the theoretical exploration. That's why I always say that "experience comes first." You must first have an experience in your body, in your heart, and in your mind. Then you can begin to understand.

It is vitally important to eat a healthy diet, to exercise and to breathe properly. No one can avoid the necessity of watching the activity of their mind and learning how to direct truthful, positive thoughts. Your heart too. Emotions running wild is not balance.

Yes, feel what you are feeling as fully as possible, but bring balance by expressing positive emotions. Let the illusory thoughts flow without trying to get rid of them but also create truthful, positive thoughts. You can learn and practice these balancing skills during the course of daily living to increase your holistic awareness and embrace a different identity. Increasingly, you will experience yourself being the "witness" who chooses balancing behaviors rather than a character who unconsciously surrenders to excessive imbalance just for short-term enjoyment.

Begin with a Self-Diagnostic

Most of us know from experience that the most difficult step in any journey is the first one. Breaking inertia takes some sort of commitment. In this case, the first step is to be truthful with ourselves. Take an honest look at the condition of your body, mind, and heart. Where are you on the balance scale? Physically, this relates to diet, exercise, and breath. Mentally, consider how your mind is functioning and what percentage of your thoughts are negative or positive, illusory or truthful, during an average day. Diagnose your emotional ratios the same way. Changing habits is difficult until you have something pleasurable to aim towards. That's why most New Year's resolutions fail. They are usually framed towards getting rid of something, like excess weight by working out or not eating donuts. Positive initiatives are more successful, as long as it doesn't take so long for the rewards to show up that you lose hope.

Again, this is why I emphasize experience as the priority and it's why I've included the High-Tech Meditation CD with this book. The motivation to balance your system comes from experiencing the rewards of doing it. That reward is the delight of consciousness, ever present and available but not consistently experienced until you learn how to live in balance.

High-Tech Meditation helps to create an environment that increases balance on all three levels. It balances the brain to encourage more positive thoughts, it balances the body by relaxing the physiology (immediately reducing stress), and that encourages emotional balance because it feels so good.

The Real Secret to Your Success

There is one human tendency that can be found at the heart of every problem we struggle with, large or small: impatience. People hurry, they cut corners, they just don't have time. And why is that? There are financial reasons, value choices, and pressure from others, but at the heart of impatience is a primary disempowering belief: we believe that we are temporary. Without life guidance from those who know differently, we have identified with our human thinking/feeling self in a body that obviously **is** temporary. While we may avoid thinking about it, we know that somewhere down the road (a destination that is approaching faster every year), death is approaching us. So, we hurry through our brief lives, looking over our shoulder at this nearing shadow. And we are afraid.

Death follows birth, but life is eternal. The multi-dimensional reality you are, in truth, simply cannot be contained between birth and death. The fullness of your life does not begin and end on that linear path, but your human instrument does. It's like your car, useful for navigating this dimensional highway. But you are the driver, not the car. As you abide in the balance point between polarities, not just in meditation but increasingly throughout your day as you practice the Holistic Lifestyle, you will connect with and experience the reality of who you truly are, beyond birth and death. Fear will flee. Love will swell in your heart. Mental storms will quiet as you direct truthful, positive thoughts and your body will balance into equilibrium. You will find yourself being happy for no reason at all, simply because you are experiencing the delighting nature of consciousness itself. Once that happens, you will be motivated to learn how to "pause-in-action," regardless of how busy you may be.

Since your fulfillment is arising from this "space," why would you hurry through it? Knowing what you now know, how could you be tempted away by anything from the physical dimension? How could you be seduced again, when you are now basking in a delight that did not and cannot originate from there?

When you sustain the experience of consciously "being," at the balance point as a daily practice over a long enough time, you grow your experience to a shift point. This is quite a moment. You will suddenly get it. You will understand that **you** are actually bringing the fulfillment you are enjoying. First, you realized that you were not getting it from your external environment, but now you realize that you are not even getting it from that balance point. You are bringing it, not getting it. Actually, you **are** the fulfillment you have been seeking, because you are One with Source Consciousness. This may have been an appealing theory – perhaps for years! – but this is now, finally, what you are **experiencing** in that balance point. This conscious knowing does not come overnight, but it will never come if you don't practice. This is a fulfillment that can last forever.

Part Six

The Power
of Holistic Living

Part Six
The Power of Holistic Living

Choosing Fulfillment

Making a commitment always unleashes unknown forces that support success. Your choice to begin meditating with the enclosed CD and study these materials so that you can apply the principles in your life is a commitment that says, "I'm serious about creating fulfillment." Universal consciousness hears that and will support you to learn how to balance your physical, emotional and mental experience. That is how fulfillment comes through the Holistic Lifestyle – a daily, momentary practice of balancing between the two relative polarities (outer and inner, action and stillness). As balance increases, you increasingly enjoy the centerpoint of delighting consciousness that resides in the space between.

Imagine not needing external stimulation of any kind to be happy. The reason people use drugs or alcohol, get addicted to unconscious sex, overwork, overplay, etc. is because they are unfulfilled. It's natural to seek fulfillment; the difference lies in where we look. Finding fulfillment by living at the balance point through the Holistic Lifestyle brings liberation. Anyone who experiments enough to achieve even a sliver of true experience gets hooked! And why not? It's what we've been looking for in all the wrong places.

Stimulants like drugs and alcohol alter your state very quickly; just as quickly, you become dependent on them. With a holistic practice you learn how to alter your own state, without needing external help. If you are able, begin reducing the use of external stimulants as a part of your commitment. Notice when you reach for something to make you feel better. That's a choice moment. Observe what you do. Remember, awareness always precedes change. Next comes the choice to make a behavior shift, to change a habit. Weaning yourself from substitutes lets you begin to enjoy the real thing. When you make a commitment to true fulfillment, you are choosing to experience the bliss of consciousness, over what any external stimulant can give you. It's well worth it!

You Can Get There From Here

We've all heard the statement that a journey of 1,000 miles begins with a single step. Before you take that first step, it helps to know two things: where you are and where you are going. As far as learning how to practice the Holistic Lifestyle goes, "Where you are" is your current reality - how balanced you are in the three aspects of your daily experience. "Where you are going" is the balance point and full experience of delighting consciousness. Initially, that's an unknown, just a theory. But you get a beginning sense of it as you meditate with the CD. Experience always precedes understanding.

Balancing the Three

Details about how to precisely balance your body, mind, and emotions are provided in my book *Forgiving the Unforgivable*[1] and other materials offered on our web site, www.synchronicity.org.

What follows here is an introduction and an overview.

Your Physical Level

The body is often referred to as "the temple of the spirit" but, for that to really mean anything, we need to treat it that way. Diet is obviously important, as is exercise, breathing, rest and sleep. But fulfillment does not come from any of these physical activities. They simply help you experience the balance point of consciousness... that's where true fulfillment arises. Everything you do is just a means to that end.

The Holistic Diet

A moderate diet of fruits and vegetables (lightly cooked or raw), healthy proteins, some fat and complex carbohydrates and very little sugar, caffeine or alcohol, with adequate amounts of water taken separate from meals, is the starting point. Reading that description, how would you rate your current diet? Are you creating balance or imbalance with what you eat? If this simple diagnostic alerts you to imbalanced diet habits, adjust. For instance, if you are eating chocolate bars every day, drinking three cups of coffee but next to no water, and vegetables have become strangers, you are creating physical imbalance. You can change that. Or, you can wait for disease to "strike" and then take your chances with the medical system.

Exercise and Breath

How much exercise do you get in the average day? Exercise oxygenates our bodies; it's as important as what we eat. Medical science recommends a good forty-five-minute cardiovascular workout every day. That is the most basic maintenance requirement. If you are choosing fulfillment through balance, then you will incorporate that into your daily practice.

We breathe constantly, yet generally fail to take advantage of the balancing opportunity that breathing – which clearly demonstrates the two relative polarities in action – provides. Out-breath represents the negative, objective polarity while in-breath is the positive, subjective polarity. If your out-breath is longer, which it is for most people, there is imbalance. This is easy to correct by deliberately increasing the in-breath.

You can use your meditation time to practice, balancing out the time of your in and out-breaths. The space between the breaths - the midpoint where the in-breath changes to the out-breath or the out-breath changes to the in-breath - is your true center. When you experience yourself living in this center, your holistic witness consciousness expands. This is the eternal here and now. Imagine living in this place consistently. This is the place of fulfillment, and all it takes to achieve more permanent residence there is consistent practice. What could be easier than using your breath to do it?

Rest

Some people do well with six hours of sleep a night, while others need eight or even nine. Some people nap every day. Some sleep less most of the time and then catch up with longer periods when they have the chance. We are all different and our needs change throughout our lives. You probably know your own biorhythms; it's just a matter of adjusting your lifestyle to get the rest you need.

I recommend meditating briefly before sleep to set up the meditative EEG in your brain. The brain retains patterns that are associated with specific experiences. When you meditate just before you sleep, you link two patterns – your waking meditation and your sleep. Your brain selects from what's available on the menu and - expecting sleep - links up a meditative EEG. There is not that much difference between sleep and meditation, so establishing the meditative EEG pattern before sleep is relatively easy and renders sleep a meditation, complete with all its benefits.

Balancing Your Emotions

Ask yourself, "How do I feel, right here and now?" Are you worried, fearful, and negative? Or are you feeling relaxed, happy, and positive? Based on this emotional diagnostic, you can create balance. If negative feelings are dominant, which they often are (and most people are not conscious of that), then you can emphasize the opposite to create balance. This is not denial. You acknowledge and experience the negative. You just don't leave it at that. You consciously, deliberately, arbitrarily express positive feelings. All feelings stem from two master emotions: love (the positive) and fear (the negative). On the positive side we list compassion, contentment, joy, gratitude, forgiveness, and more. The negative list includes anger, hatred, resentment, greed, jealousy, and more. You can train yourself to be alert and notice what you are feeling, moment to moment. If it's negative, you can make a choice to immediately express the opposite. For instance, you can balance worry with a conscious choice to focus on the feeling of contentment. It might help to use your imagination and visualize sitting by the beach or in a forest on a quiet day with sunlight filtering through the trees.

The idea of consciously creating a feeling is novel to many people; they have only experienced feeling reactively, that is, in reaction to something. Proactive emotion is something entirely different because you are the author of it. We sure didn't learn this in school or from our parents! The norm is to react and most people simply don't realize that there is any alternative. Something happens in your environment and it produces a certain feeling. But that doesn't need to be the end of the story. You can also choose to meet that reactive feeling with your own proactive one. Yes, feel what comes up, that's important. But balance it with something of your own choice. As foreign as this concept may seem and as unaccustomed as you may be to doing it, practice and repetition can help you develop and integrate this as a new habit.

Balancing Your Thoughts

Your thoughts affect your physical body and your emotions. The mental dimension has its two polarities, with a life-negative perspective as the dominant one. Since most people are on mental autopilot, they barely recognize this or know that there is an alternative. The same balancing act applies here. Start by getting conscious and observing your individual thoughts, which will acquaint you with your particular patterns of thinking. For people unconsciously identified with the content of their minds – which covers the vast majority of the human population - thinking is habitual and unconscious.

Once you recognize your thinking habits, the next step is to acknowledge that you are creating them. This is what allows you to change them. You do that by expressing positive thoughts. That is, you begin to replace negative mental programming with positive programming. Using affirmations is one effective way to do this. You simply speak a positive thought to yourself, to emphasize the positive polarity. The more you emphasize it, the more substantiated it becomes in your database. Those experimenting with affirmations for the first time may feel dishonest, saying things they do not believe are true. Well, that's progress, because you have become more aware of your negative thoughts -- in this case the negative thoughts about your positive affirmations!

Yes, you are being arbitrary, expressing the thoughts you choose to express, choosing positive thoughts that balance the automatic, unconscious negative thoughts that are running moment by moment by moment. Over time, as you deliberately practice greater positivity, your thinking habits change. It's a wonderful moment when you first begin to notice yourself thinking positive thoughts without having to consciously generate them. The new practice is taking hold.

Holistic Pointers for Practicing Fulfillment

Synchronicity associates study and master various skills that enable them to enjoy their Holistic Lifestyle no matter what challenges their circumstances may bring to them. This is the beginning of authentic leadership, where an individual can help others improve their experience, based on their own results. What follows is a brief introduction to a holistic perspective on fulfilled living in specific areas and with enough information for you to begin experimenting on your own. Of course, it's always helpful to have a coach or mentor when you are learning new skills; but, since experience precedes understanding, I encourage you to explore. These suggestions are simple and straightforward... but useless unless they are practiced consistently.

True Conflict Resolution

Conflict always starts with the individual. Conflicted individuals create conflicted relationships; conflicted relationships create conflicted families; conflicted families create conflicted societies; conflicted societies create conflicted nations; conflicted nations create a conflicted world. Obviously then, if conflict in the world is to be resolved, it must be resolved first at the individual level. As obvious as this "equation" is, it's usually ignored in favor of mediating issues without addressing the personal issues of the mediators. It's no wonder then that our world remains as conflicted as it is, with approximately 100 wars being waged at any given time regardless of all the well-intentioned efforts to bring peace. The world situation is always an accurate mirror of the individuals populating it. How could it be otherwise?

You change the world by changing yourself. Gandhi said it well: "Be the change you wish to see in the world."[2] Amazing! He said it, he modeled it, he is lionized for it, yet almost no one follows his lead and does it. Sadly, this is the case with most leaders. Christ advised that we should love our enemies. He could not have put it in clearer language. Yet how many Christians, professing that they follow Christ, hate their enemies? The hypocrisy would be humorous if it were not so tragic. "Be the change you wish to see in the world!"

Find the balance within yourself first. Resolve your own conflict. Then, to the degree that you are balanced and whole, bring that into the world and into all your relationships. Of course, most people hope to get their fulfillment from their relationships, but we are not in relationship just to make each other happy. If that's the hope, disappointment and... yes, **conflict**... is waiting around every corner. You can vouch for that in your own experience, can't you? Authentic relationship -- conscious relationship -- is meant to be a journey of mutually empowering and increasing wholeness. It is where two unique individuals support each other to increasingly know their oneness – as individuals and together - in Source.   That's something far beyond attempts at "resolving issues" while remaining separate.

The Trap of Romance

Most romantic relationships begin unconsciously.   Physical attraction strikes like lightning and two people "fall in love".   It feels great but how long does it last?   Until the honeymoon is over, which often happens before marriage!   Of course, that euphoric quick start was often fueled by alcohol or drugs, and things can feel and look profoundly different "the morning after!"   Sadly, one disappointing encounter follows another, eventually leaving many people discouraged that they will **ever** find the right person.   Of course, it's not about finding the right person, it's about being the right person yourself and supporting others to be just as authentic.

Here is a radically different way to begin a hopefully-fulfilling relationship.   Start by noticing exactly who you have attracted.   Take the time to ask yourself some simple but important questions.   Do you share the same values?   What is your comparative history like, in terms of family, career, other relationships, beliefs, etc?   Is there a reasonable possibility for balance, wholeness, harmony, growth and transformation between you?   What are the compatibilities, incompatibilities, shared values, etc?

Dare to ask the tough questions.   What might I not know about this person?   What could sabotage the beginning relationship?   What am I choosing to ignore or deny (like, he's already married!)?   These are the kinds of questions we rarely, if ever, ask, perhaps because we just don't want to know the answers! They would interfere with our spontaneous bliss. Also, there is often an unconscious hope that the chemistry will instantly (or eventually) sweep away all those annoying realities.

But knowing as much as possible about each other at the outset helps you disconnect from the projections and relate to a real person. Most of us fall in love with our projections that someone is able and willing to carry for us. Have you noticed how people seem to change over time, once you "really get to know them?" Do they really change all that much or is it your changing perception as the projections fall away to reveal who they were all along?

Early clarity creates a greater likelihood for success. All this may sound coldly logical rather than romantic, but being sensible doesn't require denying the good feelings. Let's enjoy each other as much as possible! But let's also use our wonderful thinking and intuitive capacities to learn just who we are relating with. It's an investment towards long-term compatibility and growing fulfillment together.

Of course, almost nobody takes the time to do this, which explains why the divorce rate is well over fifty percent in this country. Those who try some version of what I am suggesting are surprised to find that romance isn't stifled. In fact, with a strong foundation, romance has support to grow over time, rather than crumble.

The Illusion of Soul Mates

Some people are earnestly searching for their "soul mate" to live happily ever after together. Unfortunately, decades of research and hard-to-ignore evidence more or less proves that human beings are not monogamous. If you are hoping, even unconsciously, to find "the one and only" as you enter a relationship, it creates tremendous pressure and sabotage. Those who have managed to stay together a long time have either chosen to stay superficial and avoid their conflict that way or they are genuinely supporting each other to continue evolving and changing (rather than clinging to the way they were when they met).

If you truly want to find and be with a partner, or if you are already partnered and want to improve your experience together, invest in your own wakefulness first. Seeking from another what you don't have yourself just perpetuates your not having it. Balance your own state first. Be still, watch, meditate and witness someone drawn to your frequency because their own frequency resonates with yours. He or she might even be the one you are already with, coming close to you in a whole new way. Birds of a feather...

The path of committed, primary relationship is not for everyone. It requires a full-time focus to sustain. That's why so many relationships fail in our culture; partners simply don't invest enough in them. The relationship becomes a low priority when people get busy.

Orgasm and Lasting Fulfillment

Sexual orgasms bring you crashing into the here and now. The experience is so all-consuming that you can't avoid being present... the moment becomes everything. The radical bliss of physical orgasm is overwhelming enough to totally absorb the mind. In fact, orgasm stops the mind and this is one reason why people crave it so much. When you experience simultaneous orgasm with another person, it generates an exquisite fulfillment in oneness. The whole of your being floods with biochemical, hormonal and neurochemical releases, more pleasurable than any drug can create.

As we know, orgasm doesn't last. And what goes up must come down, often crashing down. The orgasm hangover provides fertile ground for arguments, as the blissful energy of union is replaced by the disappointment of loss. Spiritual Masters approach sexual experience very differently. They embrace sexuality as another form of meditation on the road to true spiritual intimacy, as the seeming two merge into the truthful one.

The simplest way to bring this spiritual intimacy into your sexual experience is to slow down. Focus your attention on now, rather than later, being together rather than the hoped-for orgasm to come. Be fully present for your partner, as wakeful as you can be, and release your expectations. True intimacy is the play of consciousness, so relax into the stimulation and see how far you can go without a physical orgasm. Remember that it's the journey, not the destination, that brings sustained fulfillment. Your sexual experience, especially your attitudes towards orgasm, will very likely mirror how you pursue fulfillment in the rest of your life. Make a change here in this intimate area of your life and expect to see reflections elsewhere.

Work is Love Made Manifest

Why do you work? Of course, all of us need to make a living. But is your paycheck the primary reason you go to work each day? Blessed is the individual who is doing what they do for love **and** getting paid to do it. That should be the norm for all of us but, in truth, it is only that way for the happy minority.

Work is not separate from who you experience yourself to be. Again, if you expect to "get" something – in this case from your work – then instead of bringing fulfillment, you are showing up in lack and expecting to get what's missing. In truth, your work is just another expression of the flow of your consciousness which is, remember, innately delightful. This means that if your working experience isn't full of joy, the problem is not with your job, it's in you. Work is not an obligation, it is another expression of who you are, a way you are bringing your gifts into the world. That should be fulfilling in itself, not just for the rewards it brings back to you. Synchronicity associates who have changed their beliefs about work and embraced this attitude have reported all sorts of remarkable results. Everything from the job itself suddenly seeming more enjoyable and sometimes even finding new work that was more suited to what the person loved to do. In these cases, that didn't happen because they rejected what they were doing -- they just grew out of it. They filled it so full with their expression of delighting consciousness that something additional simply had to be created. The abundant inner state of consciousness reflected itself as an evolving outer circumstance.

Money

Everything is consciousness and that includes money. All your stories about money are just stories and, if you take them away, money simply is what it is. Money has become the ultimate measure of value in our society. It's not, of course, and was never meant to be. It was designed as a convenient way to keep track of resources, not as a thing in itself. In our civilization we all need money to survive, but money is just another reflection. It is not more important than consciousness. Obviously, because you actually **can't** take it with you! Money and all other external measures of wealth are impermanent, whereas consciousness is eternal. Those who do not know that often prostitute their values for money.

Consider how wealthy you are without any money at all. For instance, you are rich enough to have the time to read this book! You are probably not dodging bullets right now, freezing to death, or drowning in a tsunami. You are privileged, blessed, and abundant, even with the challenges in your life. Breathe in your good fortune and exude gratitude as you exhale. Feel yourself awash in plenty and know that "as you give, so you receive". The money you need, all that you need to survive and thrive in this human world will come to you, magnetically drawn by the intention you express in your consciousness. Living in balance on the inside creates a healthy balance sheet on the outside and that's the holistic bottom line.

The Rewards of Balance

Wholeness is the reward for living in balance and the true measure of wholeness is self-awareness. When your awareness expands, you become more whole. That's enjoyable! Hopefully as you read this chapter, which directs your awareness towards a variety of very practical aspects of every-day living, you are feeling that expansion of awareness. As you grow in this way, your happiness, your joy, your bliss increases. You begin to find that you are happy for no reason at all, simply because you are alive and experiencing your value in being, not doing. In fact, you don't have to do anything or have anything to feel happy.

You can prove this to yourself right now. Pause as you are reading, perhaps right in the middle of a word... Reading again, slow down. Enjoy going slowly, being aware as you read and enjoying that awareness, rather than treating your awareness as a means to an end - like understanding. Instead of reading in order to understand, just read for the joy of reading, for the joy of being alive and aware in the moments of your reading. Just be, and read while you are being. Re-read this last paragraph if you wish, to repeat the experiment of enjoying your awareness. As I wrote above: "When your awareness expands, you become more whole." Being more whole means being more fulfilled and that is the point of this adventure. Finding fulfillment is really bringing fulfillment, and that is the tangible result of adopting the Holistic Lifestyle.

Fulfillment, arising from the inside, is what we then take into every aspect of our daily lives. We studied a few of them such as relationships, career, etc. But you can contemplate every activity you undertake from day to day and every relationship you have. The same imperative applies. As you learn to live in balance by consciously balancing your physical, emotional and mental levels – in the very practical ways outlined – you will expand your awareness and shift your identity from one who seeks fulfillment to one who is expressing and experiencing it.

You experience what you express -- that is the law. As you express the fulfillment that is natural to consciousness, you experience it. The search is over, leaving only the enjoyment of unending expansion and growth in consciousness… which inevitably produces ever-expanding fulfillment in living.

࠘

Part Seven

Getting Started

Part Seven
Getting Started

New knowledge must be applied to create new experience; then new experience generates expanded understanding. Trying to convert knowledge directly into understanding by leap-frogging over experience produces only intellectual enlightenment. Lasting wisdom is the result of **experiencing** new knowledge.

You may have already listened to the enclosed CD. It is provided, not as "added value" for the book, but as an essential experiential component and the way to integrate what you have read into understanding, through experience.

How to Use the CD

The enclosed CD is a sixty-minute Synchronicity High-Tech Meditation soundtrack that includes Synchronicity Holodynamic Vibrational Entrainment Technology (HVET), also known as Synchronicity Sonic Technology, operating in the Theta range. It is designed to deliver The Synchronicity Experience, whole-brain synchrony and holistic awareness through balance, an actual experience of what the words you have been reading describe. Track One is a thirty-minute musical meditation soundtrack and Track Two is a thirty-minute ocean-only soundtrack. Begin with Track One and progress to Track Two. They may also be used independently based on personal preference.

Stereo headphones are required to enjoy the full experience.

Adjust the volume to a comfortable listening level and then sit comfortably with closed eyes. Notice your breathing without struggling to change it. Be aware of any thoughts that may be circulating without trying to get rid of them. As thoughts arise – which they will – gently redirect your attention back to the soundtrack.

In our activity-burdened world, it is difficult for some people to understand how "doing nothing" could have any tangible value. Just sitting, listening to this soundtrack... how could that contribute to any productivity in your life? In fact, every moment of High-Tech Meditation balances the two hemispheres of your brain, entraining you into whole-brain synchrony. Since you obviously use your brain all day long, this means that High-Tech Meditation time can impact every moment of your ongoing existence.

The soundtrack lasts for an hour but you don't need to meditate the full hour, especially at the beginning. Always conclude by turning off the program, removing your headphones, and meditating silently without the soundtrack for several minutes. This helps you integrate your experience, and you transition smoothly back into external activity.

Some people find it valuable to begin a meditation journal to capture the insights that often arise. If you choose to do this, have your journal and pen close at hand so you can begin writing immediately following the meditation. Meditators who journal are often amazed to go back and read what they wrote months earlier and notice how ideas have grown into new experiences. Some ideas conceived during meditation are like seeds, planted in the fertile ground of your consciousness and nourished by the soothing sounds and balancing technology, eventually germinating to grow and flourish in your life.

Living the Holistic Lifestyle begins with and centers in daily meditation; but every moment of the day offers the opportunity for physical, emotional, and mental balance, which increasingly connects you with the truth of your own spiritual essence. This is the ultimate practicality of what we call Modern Spirituality – you expand your own enlightening experience by balancing your three human dimensions moment by moment by ever-present moment... and not by reaching for the heavens of obscure *esoterica*.

The Synchronicity Foundation for Modern Spirituality provides materials to support your growing experience of balance as you practice the Holistic Lifestyle and these are detailed on our web site at:

www.synchronicity.org

May all blessings continue to shower upon you through the ever-expanding journey of Modern Spirituality.

಄

For more information:

Synchronicity® Foundation for Modern Spirituality
P.O. Box 694
Nellysford, Virginia 22958
434-361-2323
1.800.962.2033

E-mail: synch@synchronicity.org
Web-site: www.synchronicity.org

Endnotes

Part 3

1.   C.W. Cade and N. Coxhead, *The Awakened Mind* (Longmead, Shaftesbury, Dorset, England: Element Books Ltd., 1989).

Part 4

1.   Psalms 91:1 (KJV)

2.   Eknath Eastawar, *Bhagavad Gita* (Tomales, CA: Nilgiri Press, 2007), 61.

Part 5

1.   Napoleon Hill, *Think and Grow Rich*, 70th Anniversary ed. (Rockville, MD: Arc Manor Publishers, 2007).

2.   *The Secret*, video, produced by Rhonda Byrne, (Canada and United States: Primetime Productions, 2006).

3.   Bhagavad Gita, quoted in Maryse Blog, "*Shifting Gears*," Sunday, March 7, 2010.

Part 6

1.   Master Charles Cannon, *Forgiving the Unforgivable* (New York: Select Books, 2011).

2.   Mohandas Gandhi, quoted in Skip Downing, *On Course: Strategies for Creating Success in College and Life* (Boston: Wadsworth, 2001), 83.

ABOUT THE AUTHOR

 Master Charles Cannon is a leader in the field of modern spirituality, a visionary and pioneer in the evolution of human consciousness. He founded Synchronicity Foundation for Modern Spirituality in 1983 and developed the High-Tech Meditation and Holistic Lifestyle experience which have helped transform the lives of millions worldwide. His speaking engagements include: the United Nations; the World Health Organization; the National Institutes of Health; Columbia, Oxford, Tel Aviv and Bombay Universities; Westminster Abbey and the Vatican.

His primary inspiration occurred during early childhood when the Blessed Mother began appearing to him. He became a close disciple of Paramahansa Muktananda, one of the most acknowledged spiritual masters of our modern era and was ordained as a monk in the Vedic tradition. His monastic name is Swami Vivekananda Saraswati.

Master Charles and Synchronicity associates inspired world audiences in 2008 by expressing love, compassion and forgiveness rather than condemnation towards Islamic terrorists who murdered two and injured four of their group during the Mumbai terrorist attack. In the aftermath of their rescue, they created One Life Alliance, a charitable, educational organization dedicated to honoring the oneness and sacredness of life.

ABOUT THE COLLABORATING AUTHOR

Will Wilkinson has written obsessively since childhood. "I cherish the unique challenges of collaborating with contemporary wisdom keepers to discover and express an authentic voice that sings harmony into the world."

ABOUT THE ENCLOSED CD

Original music by Patrick Bernard, technology by Master Charles & Synchronicity Foundation.

Patrick Bernard is an internationally acclaimed composer and recording artist. As a full-time producer and composer of devotional music, his recordings have consistently achieved high status, winning awards and inspiring listeners everywhere with his beautiful and profound music of love. He has produced 12 records and written one book, "*Music as Yoga, Discover the Healing Power of Sound*". His recording of *Atlantis Angelis* touched the hearts of more than one half million people worldwide and is among the best sellers of devotional music of all time. *www.patrickbernard.com*